"To the World You May Be Just a Teacher; But... To Your Students You Are a HERO!

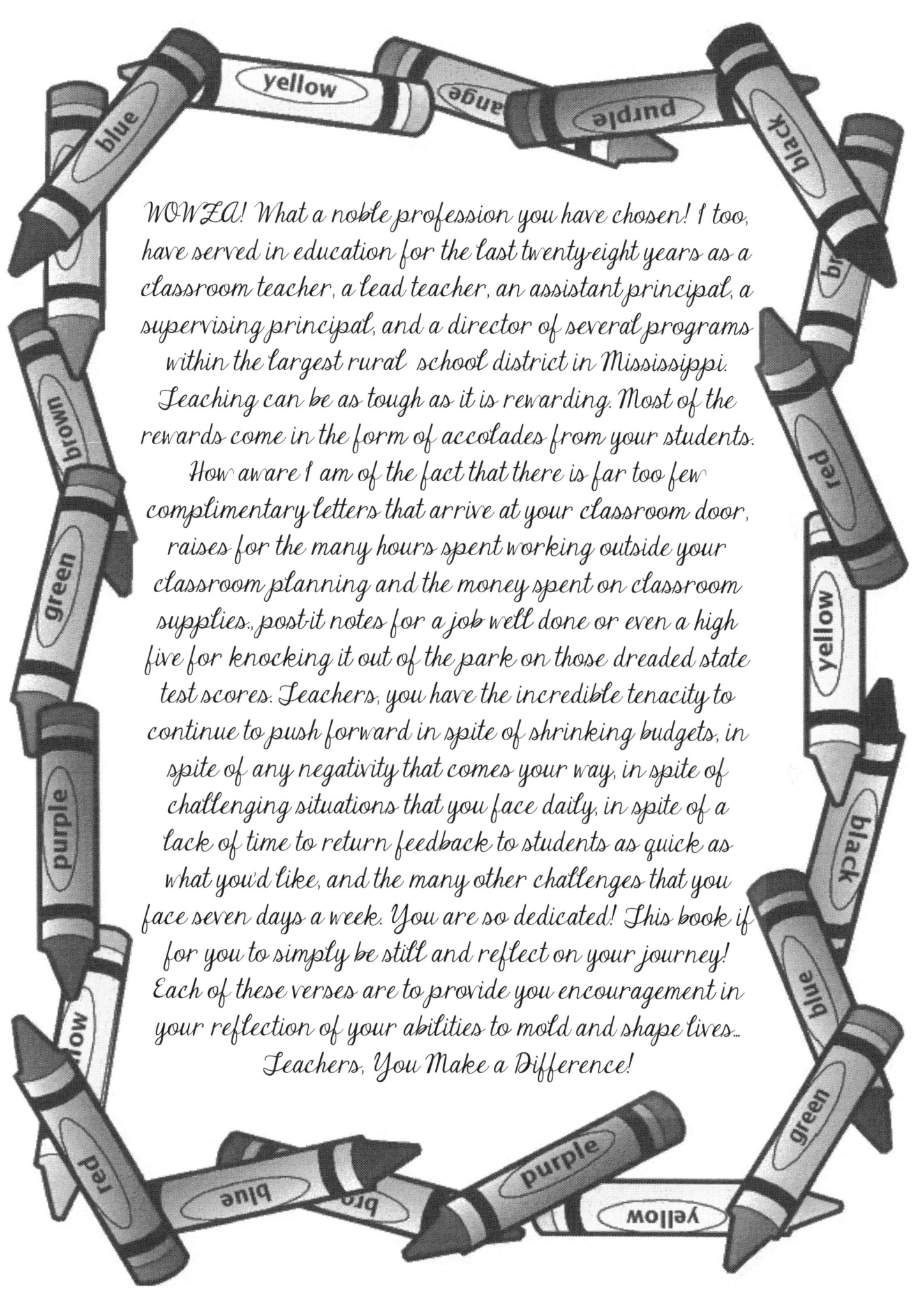

WOWZA! What a noble profession you have chosen! I too, have served in education for the last twenty-eight years as a classroom teacher, a lead teacher, an assistant principal, a supervising principal, and a director of several programs within the largest rural school district in Mississippi. Teaching can be as tough as it is rewarding. Most of the rewards come in the form of accolades from your students. How aware I am of the fact that there is far too few complimentary letters that arrive at your classroom door, raises for the many hours spent working outside your classroom planning and the money spent on classroom supplies., post-it notes for a job well done or even a high five for knocking it out of the park on those dreaded state test scores. Teachers, you have the incredible tenacity to continue to push forward in spite of shrinking budgets, in spite of any negativity that comes your way, in spite of challenging situations that you face daily, in spite of a lack of time to return feedback to students as quick as what you'd like, and the many other challenges that you face seven days a week. You are so dedicated! This book if for you to simply be still and reflect on your journey! Each of these verses are to provide you encouragement in your reflection of your abilities to mold and shape lives... Teachers, You Make a Difference!

—Suggested Materials and Resources—

- Watercolor colored pencils
- Colored pencils
- Markers
- Different colored pens
- An assortment of stamps
- Stickers
- Extra paper
- Paper towels
- Watercolor Kit
- Washi Tape
- Highlighters
- Artist Brush Pens, Basic, 6-Pack
- Big Brush Pen
- Gel Roll White Ink Pen
- Erasers
- Paints and Pastels
- Gelatos
- Alphabet Stamps
- Embellishment Stickers
- Date Stamp
- Enamel Shapes
- Paper Tags
- Misting Spray
- Tab Punch

Let's Get Started... Suggested Steps

There is no right or wrong way to journal or creatively express yourself through these verses. It is so much more about getting in God's word, reading, and reflecting on the scripture and creatively expressing meaning as a way of connecting with the scripture. The following is a suggested set of steps one might follow in the creative process of journaling these scriptures which all express encouragement for you - as you mold and shape the future

Step 1:
Read and reflect on the Scripture. In what ways does this Scripture apply to you and your life right n will focus on Proverbs 3:5-6 as our example.

Step 2:
Pick out words in the Scripture that stand out to you. Lets call them key words. For example: "trust," "Lord," "all," and "heart." These words might be ones that stand out to you more than others.

Step 3:
Think about how you visualize these words. For example, with the word "Lord," you can use very strong lettering. While with the word "heart," you might use cursive writing and add a heart around it. It's really up to you-be creative!

Step 4:
Sketch out your drawing with a pencil. You can also, of course, use a pen if you're comfortable doing so.

Step 5:
Once you have drawn over the design with a pen, use color to fill in your design. Watercolor, colored pencils, crayons or whatever else you feel comfortable with are great options for color.

Step 6:
Add any additional elements to your page that you would like. Stickers, stamps, fun borders and more will help brighten your page.

Source: http://www.lifeway.com/Article/how-to-start-bible-journaling-in-six-easy-steps

"Fix these words of mine in your hearts and minds; tie them as symbols on your hands and bind them on your foreheads. Teach them to your children, talking about them when you sit at home and when you walk along the road, when you lie down and when you get up."
--Deuteronomy 11:18-19

"I will instruct you and teach you in the way you should go; I will counsel you with my loving eye on you."
--Psalm 32:8

"Let my teaching fall like rain and my words descend like dew, like showers on new grass, like abundant rain on tender plants."
--Deuteronomy 32:2

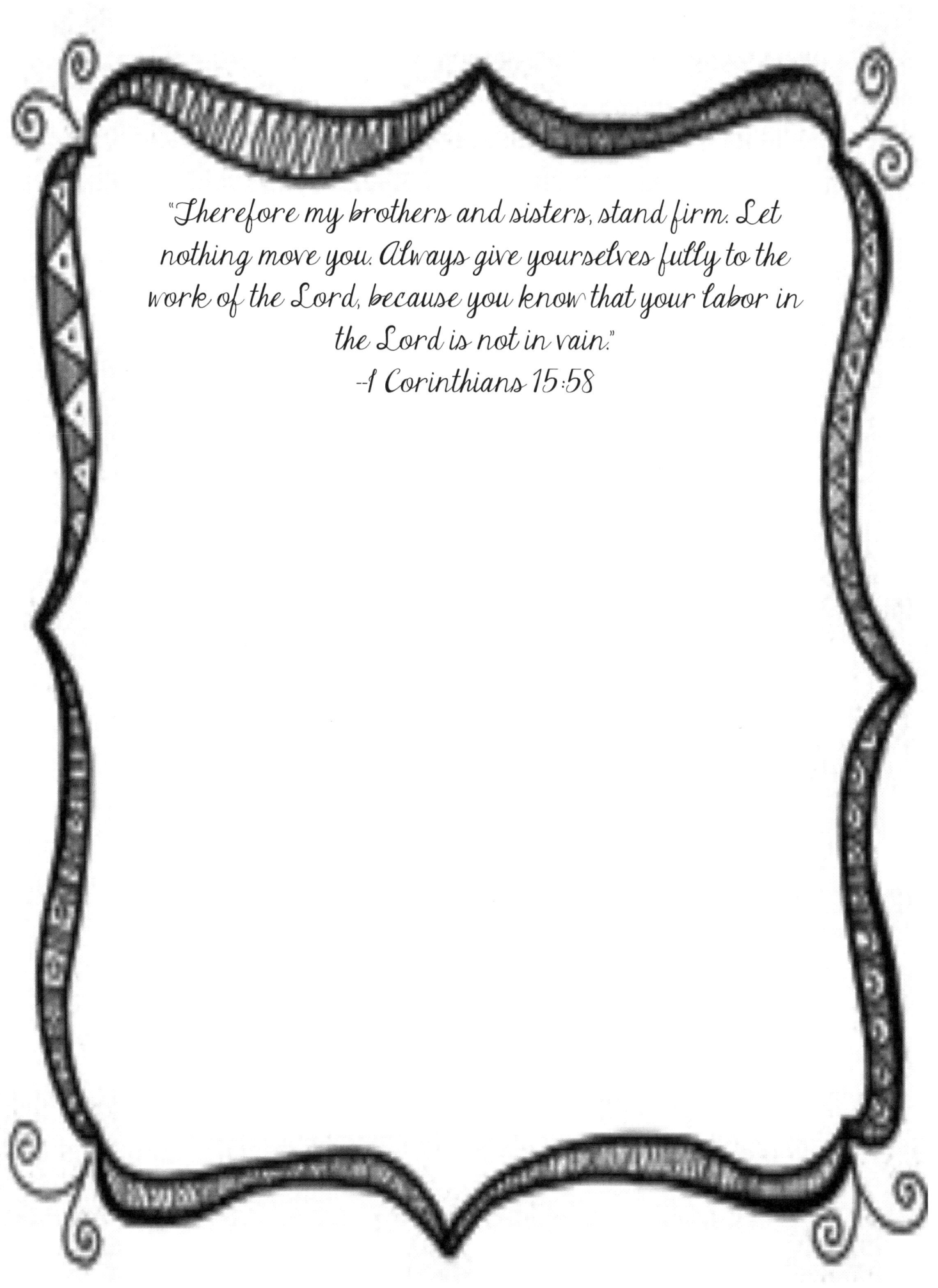

"Therefore my brothers and sisters, stand firm. Let nothing move you. Always give yourselves fully to the work of the Lord, because you know that your labor in the Lord is not in vain."
--1 Corinthians 15:58

"Young and old alike, teacher as well as student, casts lots for their duties."
-1 Chronicles 25:8

"Do your best to present yourself to God as one approved, a worker who does not need to be ashamed and who correctly handles the word of truth."
-II Timothy 2:15

"But in your hearts revere Christ as Lord. Always be prepared to give an answer to everyone to give the reason for the hope that you have. But do this with gentleness and respect.
-- 1 Peter 3:15

"We have different gifts, according to the grace given to each of us.
If your gift is prophesying, then prophecy according to your faith;
if it is serving, then serve; if it is teaching, then teach."
--Romans 12:6-7

"And of this gospel I was appointed a herald and an apostle and a teacher."
-II Timothy 1:11

"Not many of you should become teachers, my fellow believers, because you know that we who teach will be judged more strictly. We all stumble in many ways. Anyone who is never at fault in what they say is perfect, able to keep their whole body in check."
 -- James 3:1-2

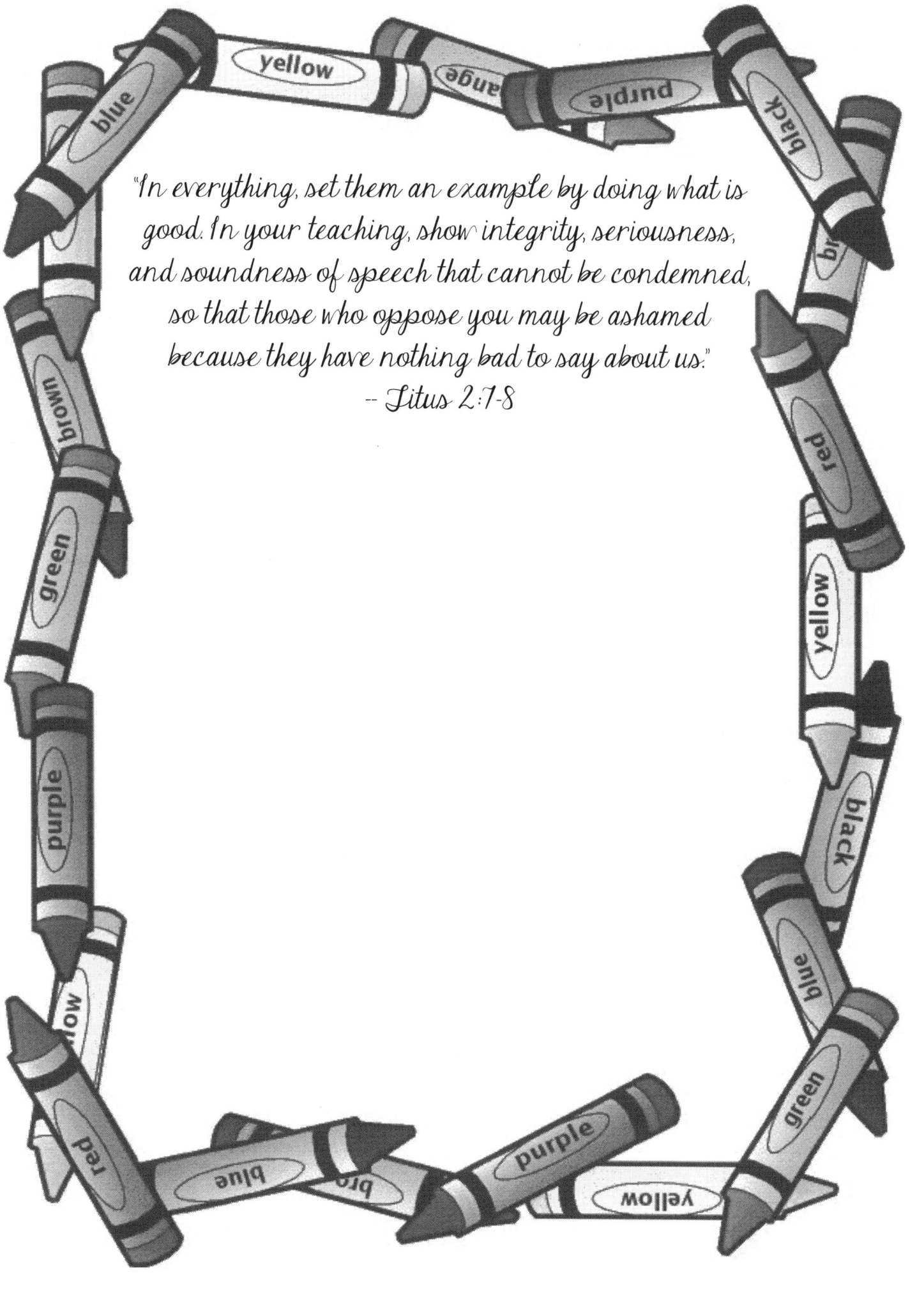

"In everything, set them an example by doing what is good. In your teaching, show integrity, seriousness, and soundness of speech that cannot be condemned, so that those who oppose you may be ashamed because they have nothing bad to say about us."
-- Titus 2:7-8

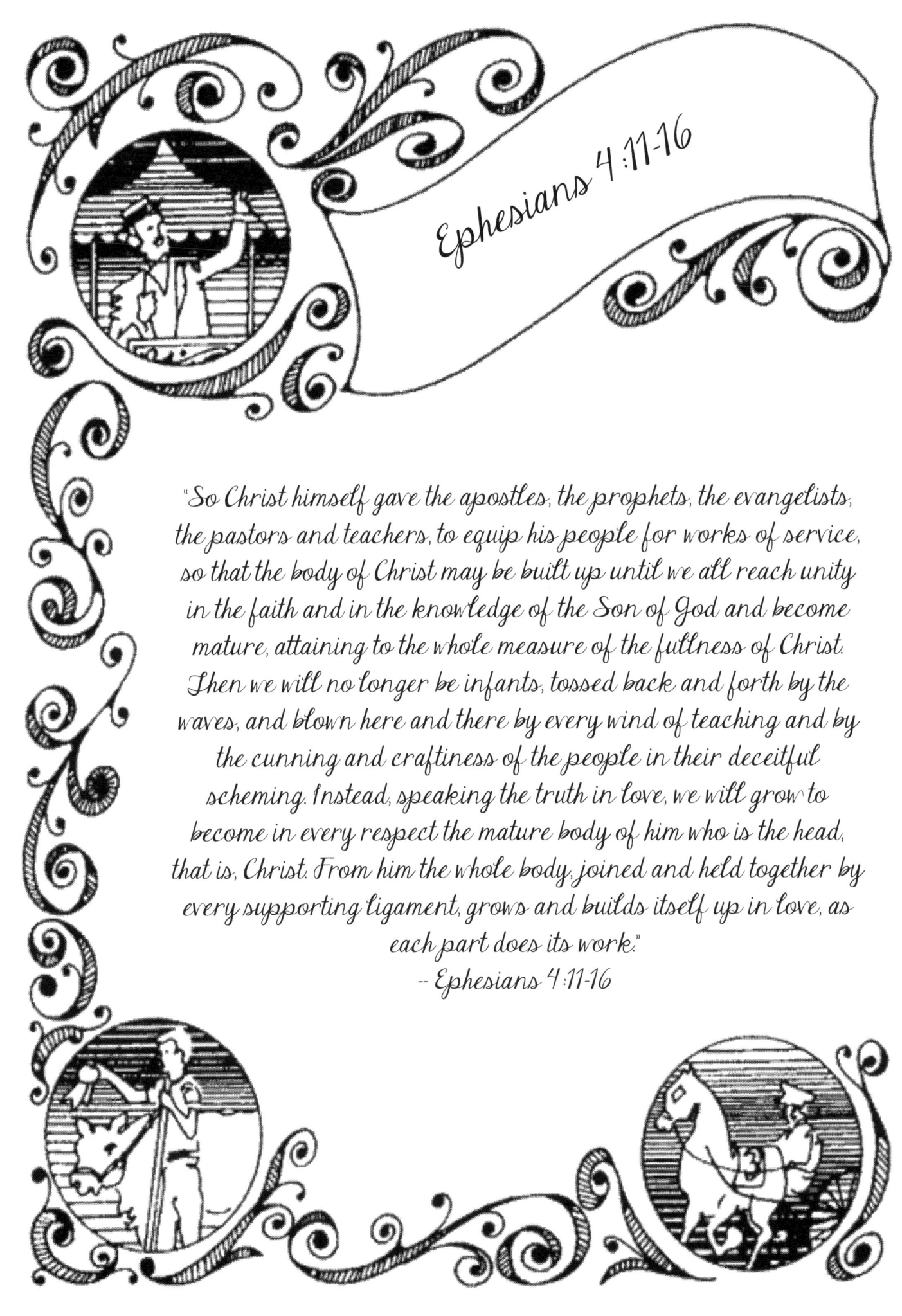

Ephesians 4:11-16

"So Christ himself gave the apostles, the prophets, the evangelists, the pastors and teachers, to equip his people for works of service, so that the body of Christ may be built up until we all reach unity in the faith and in the knowledge of the Son of God and become mature, attaining to the whole measure of the fullness of Christ. Then we will no longer be infants, tossed back and forth by the waves, and blown here and there by every wind of teaching and by the cunning and craftiness of the people in their deceitful scheming. Instead, speaking the truth in love, we will grow to become in every respect the mature body of him who is the head, that is, Christ. From him the whole body, joined and held together by every supporting ligament, grows and builds itself up in love, as each part does its work."
-- Ephesians 4:11-16

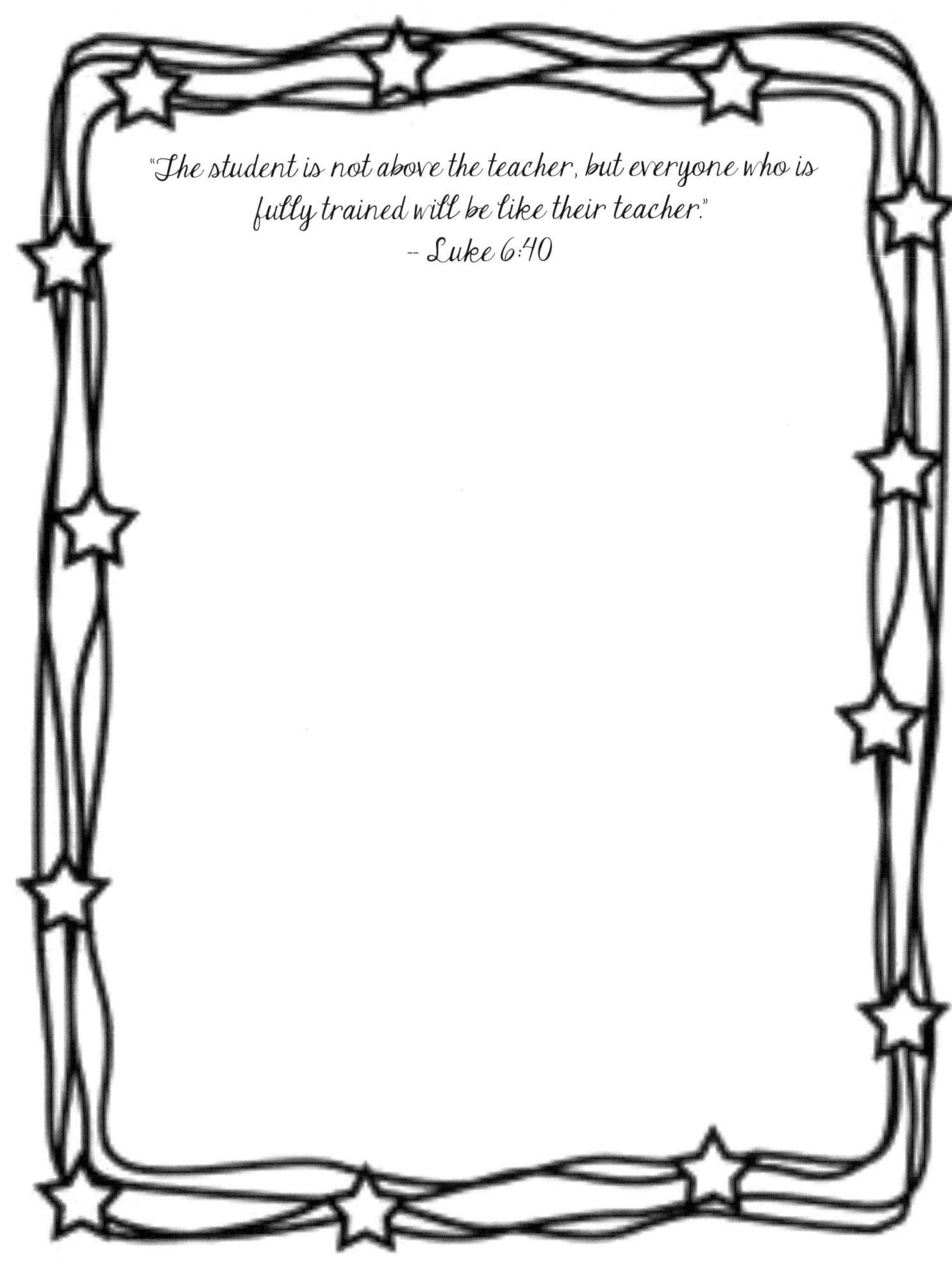

"The student is not above the teacher, but everyone who is fully trained will be like their teacher."
-- Luke 6:40

"If you know his will and approve of what is superior because you are instructed by the law; if you are convinced that you are a guide for the blind, a light for those who are in the dark, an instructor of the foolish, a teacher of little children, because you have in the law the embodiment of knowledge and truth - you, then, who teach others, do you not teach yourself? You who preach against stealing, do you steal? You who say people should not commit adultery, do you commit adultery? You who abhor idols do you rob temples? You who boast in the law, do you dishonor God by breaking the law?"
--Romans 2:18-23

Romans 2: 18-23

"Her children arise and call her blessed; her husband also, and he praises her."
-- Proverbs 31:28

"Likewise, teach the older children to be reverent in the way they live, not to be slanderers or addicted to much wine, but to teach what is good. Then, they can urge the younger women to love their husbands and children, to be self-controlled and pure, to be busy at home, to be kind, and to be subject to their husbands, so that no one will malign the word of God."
-- Titus 2:3-5

"I urge, then, first of all, that petitions, prayers, intercession and thanksgiving be made for all people-for kings and all of those in authority, that we may live peaceful and quiet lives in all godliness and holiness."
--1 Timothy 2:1-2

"If any of you lacks wisdom, you should ask God, who gives generously to all without finding fault, and it will be given to you."
-- James 1:5

"Her children arise and call her blessed; her husband also, and he praises her."
-- Proverbs 31:28

"I pray that out of his glorious riches he may strengthen you with power through his spirit in your inner being, so that Christ may dwell in your hearts through faith. And I pray that you, being rooted and established in love, may have power, together with all the Lord's gathered people, to grasp how wide and long and high and deep is the love of Christ, and to know that this love surpasses knowledge - that you may be filled to the measure of all the fullness of God."
-Ephesians 3:16-19

"Hold on to instruction, do not let it go; guard it well, for it is your life."
-- Proverbs 4:13

"Let the message of Christ dwell among you richly as you teach and admonish one another with all wisdom through psalms, hymns, and songs from the Spirit, singing to God with gratitude in your hearts.
-- Colossians 3:16

"All scripture is God-breathed and is useful for teaching, rebuking, correcting and training in righteousness."
-II Timothy 3:16

"Hold on to instruction, do not let it go; guard it well, for it is your life."
--Proverbs 4:13

Practice Page

Practice Page

Practice Page

Practice Page

Practice Page

Practice Page

Practice Page

Practice Page

Practice Page

Notes

I certainly hope that you enjoy this book, and that it allows you to express your illustrations of faith. Other books in this series include:

Other books in this series include:

Bible Journaling Workbook for Women Who Have Experienced Grief

Made in the USA
Middletown, DE
20 August 2018